HOW I SELL THOUSANDS OF PRODUCTS FROM HOME USING THE NET

Preface

Legal Information and Disclaimers

Introduction

Your Money Secret

Chapter One: Is How I Sell Thousands Of Products Using The Internet Doable or Unrealistic Hype?

Chapter Two: I still can't believe I make this much money working from home

Chapter Three: What This Course Is not About

Chapter Four: How I sell products from home over my PC using simple software

Chapter Five: How I learned the Secret of Selling Products on The Internet and Making Money

Chapter Six: I take you through my system step by step

Chapter Seven: Failing to spend the money to acquire true specialized knowledge

Chapter Eight: How I started from a shoestring

Chapter Nine: How To Come Up With Your Product Ideas

Chapter Ten: Is This Business For You?

Chapter Eleven: Everything I promised to you when you bought this course

Chapter Ten: Fifteen Tips Worth At Least $20.00

Chapter Eleven What Else Do You Need to Know

Copyright

HOW I SELL THOUSANDS OF PRODUCTS FROM HOME USING THE NET

The Preface

Dear Friend,

I want to congratulate you on your purchase.

Why?

You have purchased something that you can use again and again and will surely make you money if followed correctly. Your understanding this information is the first step in discovering an exciting and rewarding opportunity. Thousands of people the world over have profited from the information you are about to read.

For me, selling products from home via my computer has been very profitable and rewarding.

Month after month, my gross sales go up. Below is a stipend from a recent year.

January: $23,781

February: $24,739

March: $26,117

April: $26,139

May: $28,796

June: $31,116

July: $34,110

August: $37,806

September: $38,999

October: $39,999

November: $42,350

December: $48,522

I do not spend much on advertising but I am going to show you how to make the amounts above and more. If you want to make good money at home using your PC, some software and your brain, then this course will be the best investment you have made this year.

If you want to make good money with this course I suggest you read every word.

Why? If you want to pay bills, buy food, make a house payment or buy the things your kids need I suggest you read every word of this course. You will benefit most from not only understanding my methods but also my method of operation.

HOW I SELL THOUSANDS OF PRODUCTS FROM HOME USING THE NET

LEGAL INFORMATION AND DISCLAIMERS

IF THESE DISCLOSURES APPEAR EXCESSIVELY LEGAL, IM SORRY. BUT TO ABIDE BY THE LAW, I HAVE TO SAY SOME OF THIS STUFF. AS TERRIFIC AS I FEEL THIS PRODUCT IS, AS FANTASTIC THE FEEDBACK TO THIS PRODUCT IS, AS I AM REALLY EXCITED THAT YOU ARE BUYING IT, THERE ARE CERTAIN DISCLAIMERS I HAVE TO MAKE.

ALL CLAIMS OR REPRESENTATIONS MADE IN THIS PRODUCT ARE CONSIDERED EXCEPTIONAL RESULTS BY INDIVIDUALS WHO ACTUALLY USE THE INFORMATION, NOT JUST READ THE INFORMATION AND THEN THROW IT OUT, OR DO NOT APPLY THE INFORMATION, OR THE AVERAGE RESULT OF ANYONE WHO BUYS THE PRODUCT. FOR EXAMPLE, BECAUSE SOMEONE I KNOW GETS 10,000 HITS FROM ADVERTISING IN EZINES DOES NOT MEAN THAT EVERYONE WHO ADVERTISES IN EZINES WILL GET 10,000 HITS. ONLY THAT IT IS POSSIBLE.

THE REFERENCE TO THE HOW I SELL THOUSANDS OF PRODUCTS FROM HOME USING THE INTERNET HANDBOOK MEANS THE FORMULAS PRESENTED IN THE HANDBOOK AND THE HANDBOOK WORK FOR ME AND MY CLIENTS. IT DOES NOT GUARANTEE OR EVEN IMPLY THAT IT WILL WORK FOR YOU OR THAT YOU WILL BE ABLE TO DUPLICATE MY RESULTS. I CANNOT REPRESENT THIS SINCE I DO NOT KNOW YOU, WHAT YOU AIM TO DO, OR YOUR BUSINESS. I CANNOT IMPLY THAT THE AVERAGE PERSON WHO BUYS THIS PRODUCT WIL BE ABLE TO CREATE A WINNING WEBSITE OR MAKE A $100,000.00 DOLLARS ON THE INTERNET. THIS IS ONLY A GUESTIMATE AND MEANS THAT IT IS POSSIBLE.

I CANNOT IN ANY WAY MAKE ANY CLAIMS OR STATEMENTS ABOUT THE AMOUNT OF TIME IT WILL TAKE YOU TO IMPLEMENT THE STRATEGIES IN THE HOW I SELL THOUSANDS OF PRODUCTS FROM HOME USNG THE INTERNET HANDBOOK. PEOPLE LEARN DIFFERENTLY.

YOU MUST RECOGNIZE THAT ALL MARKETING AND BUSINESS ENDEAVERS INVOLVES RISK. USE YOUR COMMON SENSE. OF YOUR OWN FREE WILL YOU RISK ALL CAPITAL AND MONEY SPENT IMPLEMENTING THE HOW I SELL THOUSANDS OF PRODUCTS FROM HOME USING THE INTERNET HANDBOOK AND FORMULAS.

YOU WILL NOT HOLD BEST- VALUE- ELECTRONICS, NOR DOUGLAS FITZPATRICK LIABLE OR ACCOUNTABLE IN ANY WAY FOR ANY CAPITAL OR MONEY YOU CHOOSE TO SPEND IMPLEMENTING THE FORMULAS AND CONCEPTS IN THE HOW I SELL THOUSANDS OF PRODUCTS FROM HOME USING THE INTERNET HANDBOOK. YOU AGREE THAT YOU WILL NOT HOLD BEST- VALUE- ELECTRONICS OR DOUGLAS FITZPATRICK LIABLE OR ACCOUNTABLE IN ANY WAY FOR ANY FAILURE OF THE HOW I SELL THOUSANDS OF PRODUCTS FROM HOME HANDBOOK TO DO WHAT YOU WANT IT TO DO.

HOW I SELL THOUSANDS OF PRODUCTS FROM HOME USING THE NET

Introduction

Do you want to make a living online successfully?

What products or services should you sell to make that dream successful?

What price should you charge for your products?

How do you take orders and take orders successfully?

How do you take credit card orders?

How do you deliver your products successfully?

Is there room for you online?

How do you make a really good income at this?

Why should you run a business from home and how do you do it successfully?

How do you put up a website?

All of these questions I'm going to answer in this course.

In addition to these things you bought when you purchased this course I am going to cover the following topics:

What kinds of products are the easiest to sell on the PC?

How to find products you can sell.

How and where do you find customers?

How do you collect the money for your products?

Learn how to deliver eBooks digitally—so you don't waste money and time with mailings.

Learn how to get other people to do inventory and ship physical products saving you time and money.

My 6-step sales system and formula

Learn how to get tons of people selling your products for you.

I tell you how a friend of mine sold thousands of dollars of eBooks online.

I show you how people make money with online auctions.

You don't need an elaborate website.

How to sell stuff with emails.

I show you the software I use.

How to get started.

All of the above I am going to answer in this course.

<u>Wouldn't you agree that if I accomplish all the above objectives, the price you paid for this course is well worth it?</u>

This course is really personal in that I am going to share my personal story with you about how I got started online. I am going to take you inside my 6-step sales system and show you the meat of it.

In this course you are going to learn how to choose and price products, how I get people to my website, how I get them to buy and how I follow up with additional products and services.

You will learn where to get products to sell and what makes the difference between success and failure, how to save big bucks on software and how to build your business without spending a fortune on advertising.

Would you agree with me at this time, that if you learn to do the things above by the time you finish this course, it will be the best investment you have made in years?

So this is my contract with you. I certify that after you finish this course; all the answers to all the above questions will be answered.

After this you will know if my unique method of selling online is for you, and if you want to TAKE THE NEXT STEP.

Does this sound like a deal?

HOW I SELL THOUSANDS OF PRODUCTS FROM HOME USING THE NET

Your Money Secret

Welcome to How I sell Thousands of Products using the Internet.

Congratulations! By purchasing this eBook, you have just taken a HUGE first step toward achieving financial independence in a life-changing career.

If you would like to sell products like crazy from home using your PC – without spending your life's savings – this report may be the single most important you will read this year.

Why?

Because I've sold thousands of products and services using my computer, an Internet connection, my brain and common software.

And that's only Pay Pal. That does not include my regular credit card orders and checks!

My results are exceptional! Your results can and will vary.

Of course, what I have earned is not typical of what the average person does who buys my products. I do not know if it is true or not but I am told more people who buy products in the marketing category don't make money with them in that they don't read them or they just never get around to doing anything. Only you know what you will do.

The good news is that my fixed overhead is low since I work at home, and the profits can be fantastic, considering that other people do my most marketing and advertising for me.

No other business venture costs so little to get started or is as easy to get off the ground – or can immediately start padding your wallet!

And that's why I have written this eBook – to tell you about the FASTEST, EASIEST ways imaginable to make money online!

You can earn incredible money selling products or selling other people's products, without spending a dime on inventory, storage, or shipping!

You do not have to invest in risky product development or put out a huge amount of cash to buy inventory that will never move – all you have to do is follow the system I'll show you in this book.

What you're going to find in the following pages is a proven step-by-step formula that GUARANTEES there is a market for products – before you even know what those products are!

And I am going to show you precisely how to make this proven 'dummy-proof" system work for you.

This product has 13 chapters on how to sell thousands of products on the Internet. Also I am going to teach you how to get hundreds of people selling your products for you.

This information will help you if you are trying to sell products on the internet from your own website, if you have a associate program or you have your own product to sell.

This business has been very good to me. When I first started out in this business I was broke, penniless and living in my car. Back in those days to do marketing we had to address envelopes by hand, stamp them and mail them. There were no databases, email or direct response marketing. It was an expensive way to do a business.

In the old days, we did it with direct mail. And those promotions would show up in your mailbox.

You did not have the internet when I first started learning to do this stuff. The game was you'd run these little ads in ad sheets or magazines offering a report. People would write in and then you would send them your sales letter.

Nowadays, you can do that in 30 minutes using Google AdWords. Back then, I'd run my little ad and wait 2 or 3 months for it to come out. I'd spend all the change I had trying to print up and mail stuff

Thing is, it costs quite a bit to print and mail those letters.

It costs very little to send emails.

I started doing copywriting for a publishing company where I met I two guys there named Mike Filsimaine and Declan Dunn.

I really didn't know what a cookie was or what a domain meant but when I learned what these terms were and how to apply them I began making a lot of money.

These two guys taught me a lot of things about direct response marketing and copywriting and I applied this to my own business and I began making a lot of money.

Way back when I started out in this business one had to write up sales letters by hand, put stamps on the envelopes, seal them and mails them by hand. This was an expensive proposition and then the Internet came along all one had to do is email sales letters out to people.

This was a blessing to me and I began making a lot of money.

Since people around the world buy products from me, I'm diversified in case my country's economy goes to pot.

But enough about me.

This course is about you. And how you can copy my system of selling products from home using your computer, common software – and your brain.

Do you have a home based business? Have you ever thought about starting a business? Do you have a product or service to sell? Then this could be the answer you're looking for. It has been for many others.

I am truly touched by all the letters we have received from around the world from people who have been helped by our information.

People get enthusiastic when they talk about my information and systems. Why? Because there is nothing more exciting than waking up in the morning and checking your computer to see how much money you made while sleeping that night!

Here's some info about me:

My name is Douglas Fitzpatrick. I'm 43 years old and live in a home in McKinney, Texas.

The first thing you should know about me is I go to bed as late as I want. And I sleep in almost every day.

Then, after I do wake up, most mornings I suck down some coffee, then hop online to see how many products I sold while I was sleeping then high tail it down to the gym and do 15 or 20 minutes on the treadmill.

On a lazy day, I swing by Whataburger, grab a cup of coffee, snag the newspaper out of the pile the store leaves laying around – and read the latest scoop on the Cowboys or other sports teams. Those are my favorite days because they remind me of when I had a "job." When I too had to rush to work in the morning.

It does my soul much good just to watch all those people. Hurrying around and running around like chickens with their heads cut off. I haven't done that for years. And I know it's a little twisted. But I get a secret pleasure from watching those people. Knowing that I will never – ever – do that again.

I am typing this on the same computer I use to sell hundreds of thousands of dollars of products on. It's an exhilarating business. There's nothing like selling products around the world.

I knew this was the business for me because of the super-low overhead. If you've ever owned a business or tried to start one that you lost money with you can relate to this: One time I owned a retail store. I lost money faster than you can say "get me out of this business!"

Nothing I did or tried worked.

After that dismal experience, I figured out that the way to make money is to have lots of money coming in and not very much going out. I realize this may be a stretch for you to believe that you can sell products on the Internet after all the dot com's crashed and burned.

That's the beauty of this business – it is ideal for the person who works at home or in a small office and keeps their overhead low. The reason the dot com's failed is they had massive overhead.

If you open your mind and give me a chance, I will show you how and why I'm convinced you can copy my system and create your own success story.

My Embarrassing Confession

It's a little embarrassing to admit this.

I wasted an enormous amount of time, energy and money developing my system. I always wanted to make money selling products. I just was not good at it for a long time.

For example, I once had a job selling insurance. I got one of those machines that would call people all day long and ask if they wanted free information.

I put 30,000 miles on my car in six months following up on those leads and sold only one homeowner's policy on an old, small, wooden-frame house that my company really didn't want to insure for obvious reasons. The thing was, I didn't understand WHY they were reluctant to write insurance on it! I was just happy I sold something!

I tried everything. I sold stuff door-to-door. I sold timeshare, credit card insurance, home food delivery, advertising, retirement programs – and all kinds of other things.

Times were bad then.

I will never forget. I had a date with this six-foot tall, drop dead gorgeous model. She didn't know I drove a beat-up car that smoked like it was on fire! I took her to this fancy restaurant and the valet guys were laughing until they saw her step out of the car.

Holy smokes!

Unfortunately, I never saw her again.

And there was the time I bought deodorant with all pennies (just two miles away from where I live now). The man behind the cash register said, "Normally, we don't accept all pennies. But in your case, I guess I will make an exception."

I bought every single book I could afford on marketing and selling. And some I couldn't. I literally have read thousands of books. And while I forgot a few gems (very few), most all of them were worthless. I did not know then. But I realize it now.

Why were they worthless? Because the book author didn't have a proven system or formula for selling products. And if he or she did, that information wasn't shared in the book.

It's a long story. But simultaneously two things happened: One, I stumbled across a formula for selling products that really worked. And two, I discovered selling on the computer.

It was as though I finally put two-and-two together. God knows it took enough. Anyway, in short order, my luck turned around. I was hired by a corporation involved in Internet marketing (this was before the World Wide Web existed), to write their marketing promotions. There I met my mentors who had been personally trained by an old-time mail order legend.

He mentored me as his mentor had done for him. And now it's your turn and mine. It's my turn to give back. To mentor others as I have been mentored.

I was only at the Internet company for six months or a year. Then I was out on my own. First, I sold my writing skills. Then I sold products.

When I discovered the "the secret" my gross sales were $20,000 the first month. And over $40,000 the second month.

(Remember, these results are exceptional. Your results can and will vary).

It's almost impossible to describe the feeling when my sales skyrocketed. Wow! What a rush. The first thing I did was pay off a $5,000 credit card that had been hanging over my head.

What a relief!

Since then, the sales have kept rolling in. I have spoken at over 120 seminars, where people paid $3,000 just to hear me and several of my friends speak for only one day. I say this not to impress you but to impress upon you what a difference this has made in my life.

I have spoken at Wembley arena in England where the stage design almost cost $20,000. I have spoken in Bermuda, Hawaii, Rotan and every major city in the U.S. I have been to Hong Kong, Thailand and I am going to Australia to speak at a seminar this October.

Nowadays, I mostly just sell my products on the Net using my system. I sell hundreds of thousands of dollars. Selling products on the internet is a dream come true.

I'm not the only person I know who does what I do. It's no accident. I and a number of friends in this business do very well also. In fact, some of them make my income look like child's play.

If this business is your thing, your cup of tea, I may have a big influence on your life. You may remember this day, the day you read this letter, for a long time to come.

One of the great things about this business is you can travel.

Why? Because everywhere you go, all you need to run your business is a internet connection. And you can find that everywhere. In most countries, I didn't even use my laptop. I just dropped into the Internet cafe around the corner.

Opportunity is everywhere

The question you're likely asking yourself is, "why am I willing to share this information?" Right?

The answer is simple and common sense:

One, the market is worldwide. There's room for both of us.

Two, I've devoted my business and my life to mentoring others in the system I was fortunate enough to discover. This is both my mission and livelihood.

I don't expect you take my word for it. I will prove to you I do what I say I do.

I don't expect you to take my word for this. Not at all. In a second, I will show you how you can get proof that what I say is true. And most important are you can prove to yourself it will work for you. Because that's really the test, isn't it?

It's all fine and dandy that it works for me. And I make money. But what about you? Right? Will it work for you?

That's the ultimate test. And I'm going to give you the chance to prove yourself. More about that in a second.

Now, you can prove to yourself you can sell products using my system -- without risk!

The old expression is true: The proof of the pudding is in the eating.

You will just really never know until you get my system in your hands and check it out for yourself. Then you'll know. That's why I put my system in this eBook that you can download in the next five minutes and read – risk free.

Here are just a few of the things it reveals:

- What types of products are easiest to sell on the PC
- Where to find products you can sell
- How and where to find customers
- How to collect the money for your products
- How to deliver software and eBooks digitally – so you don't have to stock anything
- How to get other people to inventory and ship physical products for you so you don't have to junk up your house
- My 6-step hyper drive sales system
- How to get dozens or hundreds of people selling your products for you
- How a friend of mine sold thousands of dollars of diamonds online
- How people make money with online auctions
- Why you don't need a big, fancy web site
- How to sell stuff with email letters
- The simple software I use
- How to get started

I have put my latest system into a tidy eBook called *How I Sell Thousands of Products From Home Using The Net!* It has all the information in it.

<u>Wouldn't you agree that if I accomplish all the above objectives, the price you pay for this course will be one of the best purchases you've made recently?</u>

This course is highly personal in that I'm going to share my personal story with you. I am going to take you inside my six-figure operation and show you the guts of it.

I'm going to tell you how we choose and price our products, how we get people to our web site, how we get them to buy, how we follow up with additional products and services – the whole process.

You will discover where to get products to sell. What makes the difference between success and failure, how to save a fortune on software, how to build your business without spending a lot of money on advertising and much more.

Would you agree with me right now, that if you learn how to do the above things by the time you finish the course, it will be the best investment you've made in a long, long time?

Then this is my contract with you. I guarantee that by the time you finish this course, you will have the answer to every question listed above.

And you will also know if my unique method of selling online is for you, if you want to take the next step.

Now listen up, there are a few things I want to make absolutely clear and to clear for legal purposes:

1. If you use my system, you may not make a dime. All business involves risk. I've got this thing down to a science as far as I'm concerned. But there are no guarantees it will work for you – other than your money loss if it doesn't.

For all I know some people who read this letter will have all the common sense of a pet rock. So obviously I can't guarantee results.

If you cannot afford to lose either time, money or both speculating in business, then you shouldn't be in business – any business. Then again when I first started in this business, I was pretty broke.

But I was willing to risk what I did have for the chance of gain.

2. I don't claim or represent the average person who buys and/or uses my system makes a red cent with it. I don't shoot for average, and I hope you don't either.

The fact is, the average person usually fails in whatever business they undertake in. That's why God invented jobs.

This system is not a "no-brainer." You still need a brain and you have to work. This is not a "win-the-lottery" system.

3. The system is simple. You do NOT need to learn something complicated. What you need is to DO something. Because the only thing that's going to make you money is SELLING a product. And the only way you do that is to follow a simple method you can actually DO!

4. This is an entry-level product for beginners. If you're looking for advanced marketing training, go to: http://www.cashlikeclockwork.com

WARNING: Do not buy any marketing course that does not meet the following criteria:

There are so many scammers and rip-off artists online; It is often confusing who you should listen to for advice. I thought it'd be helpful if I present to you a few criteria to help you only invest your dollars in stuff that's going to deliver you a great big bang for your buck:

1. Only buy from marketers who have a background in direct response marketing.

Traditional advertising agencies are clueless about direct response. They only understand image advertising and "branding." Branding is terrific if you're a $100 million dollar corporation. But if you aren't, you better know as a fact that every dollar you spend is coming back to you multiplied. My background is 100% direct response. That's what I do.

2. Do NOT buy packages that promise or imply they'll make you rich virtually overnight or make you X dollars in X time period.

For example, don't buy packages that say they'll make you $1,000 a week, $10,000 a month, $X next year, etc. Those claims are obviously bogus and the person has never met you. For all they know, you're Charles Manson. How can they claim you'll make a dime?

I cannot and do not suggest you will make even a dime with what I offer even if I have a strong money back guarantee. But it isn't based on how much money you do or do not make.

By the way, the FTC says that if you make such claims, they have to be representative of what the average person does who buys the product, unless you clearly state otherwise. This is why I usually have a full page of legal disclaimers on my products.

You should also know that the same thing applies to testimonials. You'll notice that on my testimonials I always state that they aren't meant to represent what the average person does.

3. Similarly, do not buy products that make obviously false claims.

For example, I'll guarantee you make $9,000 in only 90 days. Yeah right. I give some pretty dramatic success stories of specific techniques people I know have used. For obvious reasons, that is far different from saying do the same thing – guaranteed.

Oh, here's another one: Free bonuses with price tags that are way out of whack with reality. I've seen some pretty crazy stuff.

4. Learn from someone who has been selling online at least 5 years.

This way, you won't be learning second hand from a "Johnny-come-lately.

You can go to http://www.betterwhois.com ,type in a domain, click the "more information" link and find out when a domain name was filed.

5. Choose a mentor who has written sales letters professionally

A large part of selling on the web is your sales copy. Before selling on the web, I wrote for paid clients. In fact, I have been paid over $10,000 before to write just one sales letter. And I now get paid $1,000 an hour for consulting.

You get my complete system, the secrets of my success for only $25.99.

The question is, is it worth the $25.99 to know the secrets of selling hundreds of thousands of dollars of products from home?

You can easily waste 5 or 10 times that much money buying courses and products that are a total waste.

You can easily waste that much money just buying a bagel and coffee 5 times a week.

If you follow my system you will make money. Is it worth it to you to have a better lifestyle?

Pay off bills?

Do not have to worry about how to make your next mortgage payment so you do not lose your house?

Or worry about if you will have a job next week in this economy?

Escape shitty jobs and bad bosses and how you will feed your children?

Have more time with your children and take the vacations you always dreamed of?

Buy the house you always dreamed of?

Have a stable income month after month?

HOW I SELL THOUSANDS OF PRODUCTS FROM HOME USING THE NET

Is How I Sell Thousands of Products From Home Using the Internet Doable or Unrealistic Hype

How unrealistic and undoable is it to think that anyone can sell thousands of products from your computer from home using the Internet

We are all in disbelief and procrastinate of this idea, don't we?

We have all seen the dot com companies go under. We have all seen the bad press on the TV about dot.com companies. Some of us are surprised the Internet is still around.

But Yet, not only is the Internet still around, but the business is thriving.

By the end of 2002, more than 900 million people around the world will have access to the Web, and unbelievably they will spend more than 1 trillion dollars U.S. shopping online. Wouldn't you like to have a small piece of this?

Compare this to 600 billion in sales in 2001. Did you get that? 600 billion dollars in 2001. Is there enough room for you and your pc and your product line?

All you need to do is to suck out a little bit net from a potential market of 600 billion to make a incredible amount of money.

What do you think it takes to reach that incredible amount? Not as much as you may think.

Just sell 400 products per month with a profit of $20.00.

Or sell 200 products per month with a net profit of $50.00.

Or sell 100 products per month with a net profit of $100.00.

What I am talking about is after deducting 15% for overhead, and tax expenses. In a latter chapter I will break the numbers down more exactly.

You really have to understand that you do not need to get a whole lot of new customers each month to make the above amount. Using my 6 step system, you can make an incredible amount of money from existing customers.

I am going to show you how to make that happen automatically without a lot of effort.

The point I am trying to make is it is not as hard to make $100,000 in a year as it may seem to some. With this fact in mind don't you think it is worth shooting for?

All you need to do is create a doable simple business plan. By the end of this course you will know how to sell thousands of products and make a really substantial profit.

This is really exciting to me because I have done it. Let's move on.

HOW I SELL THOUSANDS OF PRODUCTS FROM HOME USING THE NET

I Still Can't Believe I Make This Much Money Working From Home

My name is Douglas Fitzpatrick. I'm 45 years old and single. At the time I am writing this, I am in my office in my dining room petting my cats

I am sitting at my computer listening to usher and trying to figure out additional ways I can help people make money and become successful. My life is a rewarding life in many ways. I have made a lot of money on the Internet and couched many others to do the same.

I go to bed as late as I want. Sleep as long as long as I want. Take days off. Some of my friends in this business have families and do the same. This business has been very rewarding for them because they have time to spend with their families and do not have to worry about supporting them.

In the pre-internet days it would have been impossible to do what I do now.

In the pre-internet days you had to print up and mail sales letters for the products you were trying to sell. Each of these letters cost a dollar and more to print and put in the mail. You had to spend money upfront before knowing if you would get any back and this was a risky proposition.

This was a really expensive and time consuming way to run a business.

Now all I do is type up a email and sending it out to my existing customers and prospects. A real time and money saver. If people do not buy all I am out is an email and I can contact them by email in the future.

In some cases, I am out the time to create the product but I can use email to follow up later.

The really good thing about this business is that I do not have gigantic printer bills and do not have to travel back and forth to the office supply store every time I create a printout of a product I have to offer or create a printout of emails for further marketing research. The Internet simplifies many things.

With my business I have customers all over the globe. This is a nice feeling and I do not have to worry about finances. This business has enabled me to travel all over the world and all over the United States.

In this course I am going to take you inside my operation.

I am going to teach you the things that make me money.

The only edge you have in the Information Age is – information The single most valuable commodity you can own is information.

Information in the form of what Napoleon Hill, author of the book *Think and Grow Rich,* calls Specialized Knowledge. Because information is free on the internet, some people confuse that information with specialized knowledge.

For example, say you are boarding a plane to take a trip overseas. Do you want to fly in a plane piloted by someone who read a book on how to fly a plane? No, you want to fly on a plane piloted by a pilot who has experience. You want the pilot to be someone who has gone through a real pilot training program.

You would like the real deal, don't you? You see there is a big difference between free information and specialized knowledge of a craft.

With the advent of the Internet, we now have TOO MUCH information. Un-filtered, unorganized, irrelevant information is noise. But highly specialized information that enables you to get a result is priceless.

Many people have started web sites and not made a dime with them. Others sell millions of dollars a year. What is the difference?

You could point to many things. But ultimately it boils down to one thing -- Know how.

Those who know how to make the money. The others may think they know it all. In fact they may know it all. The problem is, they do not know how to sift through the vast sea of information and focus on those things that Do make money.

The proof is in their lack of income

How much is it worth to you to know what actually works? To have a paint by numbers system you can plug your products into and make money with.

Do you want to work hard? To try and reinvent the wheel? Or do you want to plug into a success system that is already tried, tested and proven to work?

If you want a success system, then you have come to the right place. This is what this course is about.

HOW I SELL THOUSANDS OF PRODUCTS FROM HOME USING THE NET

What This Course Is Not About

To me the first step in learning is to clear your mind. I believe it is impossible to absorb new information if your mind is cluttered with a bunch of misinformation, fears and doubts. To succeed in this course you need to clear your mind.

Let's get started with those ideals right now.

1. This is not a book report on ideas I read somewhere else and I am rehashing to you. This chapter is about what I know works because this is what I do in my business every day.

2. This chapter is not about a guaranteed way to get rich or, in fact make any money at all. In business there are no true guarantees even with research. In business and especially this eBook there is the possibility of risk and loss in exchange for the potential of making money. What I can do for you are reveal how I personally make money.

3. This course is not about hitting up your family and friends to buy products from you. That is ridiculous. You can do this from the internet. You can get your own customers from the internet. This is what is really great about the internet.

4. This course is not about how to become a millionaire by spending three million dollars! In business there are always risks. It takes money to make money. With this fact in mind I'm assuming you are not a millionaire and you're starting with a minimum of working capital.

5. This course is not about everything you will ever need to know. I have found that successful people make a commitment to learning on an ongoing basis. Just learning one course can and will not do it all for you. I spend $5,000.00 or more a year on my own continuing education. Other successful people I know do the same. In education, you get what you pay for. I choose to learn from the best.

6. This course is not a way to make money with silly schemes and plans that waste your money that only amateurs participate in. There are dozens of silly schemes and plans online that I will not tell you about that waste your time and money. I do not want to waste your time with that junk.

7. This course is NOT about an impractical dream no one ever does. This course is not one of those get-rich-quick ads in magazines that paint fanciful tales that are nothing but lies. In other words, I'm not selling blue sky. You will find no silly schemes here. I am a real person. My business is real. Every year we sell thousands of products around the world.

8. This course is not about making money with no effort. If you want to do that buy a get rich quick scheme. If all you want to do is set on your rear and procrastinate do not buy this course. Selling products takes time and effort.

A challenge in starting a business is who to believe. There are many people who sell you just what you want to be sold. They portray unrealistic pictures and promise incomes that are not true.

So there you have it for this chapter. I am talking straight. No B.S.

Here we go to the next chapter.

HOW I SELL THOUSANDS OF PRODUCTS FROM HOME USING THE NET

How I Sell Products From Home Over My PC Using Simple Software

There are really only some basic steps you need in selling products and services from home using your PC.

Step one: Find a demand

You cannot sell what people do not want. All people buy what they want, not what the need.

So your first step you need to know in selling is to find a demand that already exists. I am not in the business of creating demands from scratch. This is really a expensive thing to do. Yet this is where most people screw up. Just about everyone starts with a product.

What software do you need

Like any business you need a set of tools for this type of business. These are things you must have. They're your tools. What difference does it make how much they cost? If you're going to be in business you have to have them.

GET THE TOOLS YOU NEED!

OK!! So what are the tools you need for this business. Here are the basic tools you need for this business. These include software and various services.

1. Eudora -- Free or your existing email program.

This is the program I use to read and respond to email. It is a heavy-duty email management program. You are going to be responding to lots of email. So this is a tool you need. Eudora is free and can be downloaded from the internet. Search on Eudora from any engine.

2. WinZip -- $29.00 to $39.00

If you don't have a program to zip and unzip files, then get one. This is the one I use. Mac people use a program called Stuffit. When you zip a file, you compress it and make it much smaller so you can email it or transfer it to a floppy disk or CD. WinZip zips and unzips programs for you automatically. Using it is a no brainer.

3. Front Page or Dreamweaver -- $100.00 - $300.00

If you are on a slim budget, you can buy a used copy from ebay.com. You're going to use the heck out of Front Page or Dreamweaver. This is the program you will use to design your web site with. When you type, the program converts your text to html, which is the code that web browsers read. This is all done in the background.

4. WS FTP LE -- Free

This is the program you'll use to upload your html pages to your web host. This is what makes your pages magically appear on your web site. You can download this from the net for free.

5. A graphics program -- $40.00 - $70.00

You will need a graphics program like Photoshop version 6 or 7 or Paint Shop Pro. This is what makes graphics appear on your site and makes your website look good and appealing to the customer. If you're on a slim budget, try Xara Web Style.

6. Your Internet Connection -- $20.00 - $80.00 per month

You likely already have an Internet connection or you wouldn't have purchased this course. I recommend the fastest connection you can get.

7. Web hosting -- $2 - $25 per month

This is not software but it is a tool you must have in this business. Most of our websites cost us $2.00 per month. A web host is a server that holds your website, i.e., your text and or graphics. You cannot succeed in this business without a web host. You upload your text and graphics to your web host using FTP. Some web hosts cost $80 per month and are unreliable and others cost $20 per month. Look for unlimited bandwidth. Do your research. With a little luck you can find a good one cheap. For a good starting point try http://www.therealstartpage.com/.

8. Autoresponders -- $10.00 - $40.00 per month

Autoresponders are what you follow up with your customers with and make you money. For best results you need sequential autoresponders. These follow up with your customers more than once a month so your customers remember you and make you back end sales. For good autoresponder companies go to http://www.therealstartpage.com/ where you can find good deals.

9. Merchant Account -- $20.00 - $40.00 per month plus set up fee.

You can find a good deal and save some money with http://www.revecom.com/ if you require a payment gateway. They do require you have a registered business name to use their service though. If you do not have this, just use PayPal instead. PayPal is free and is what a lot of internet marketers use.

10. Real time credit card processing -- $20.00 month plus each transaction fee

This is the service that charges or authorizes credit cards for you automatically. My processor has a minimum monthly fee. In other words, if I do not process a certain amount of transactions each month, I still pay that amount and no more. Check out ecenow.com.

11. Norton Anti-Virus Software -- $40.00 to $50.00

Norton is the anti-virus software I use. You cannot scrimp on this. You have to have it. Check your local computer store for the latest prices or search on Norton antivirus software in any search engine.

12. Phone, fax, etc.

There are other things you will need like a telephone, fax machine and printer. You can obtain a fax machine cheap off of eBay or you can buy a used one from your newspaper. You can also buy the Win fax Pro software and use your computer as a fax if you are on a limited budget.

Basically a website is a collection of text files and or graphics files you created by some means or used a computer program or typed into an existing service. You type your message or sales letter including text or graphics into the program or service or edit the program and service and then upload it to your web host using ftp (file transfer protocol).

If you want your web page to be seen by customers or anyone on the internet you need good html code. A front page program will do most of the html code for you but there are still a few things you need to add. For a good understanding of html see Chapter 1.

When creating your website using a front page program or Dreamweaver program or editing content into register.com or an existing online business website by copying from your front page program or Dreamweaver program or editing, save your home page(the page you want customers to see first when they access your site from a browser) as a .html file.

This insures that the page you want to be seen first by your friends or customers on the internet is your home page When you see http://www.amazingformula.com/ in your browser what you are seeing is your home page. When you see www.amazingformulacash.com/trivia you are seeing each individual file and or graphic you created.

As you can see, there are some minimum costs in creating a winning internet business. But you must understand, any business requires you to invest money to be successful. The thing about a internet business is I do not know of many places where you can invest this little amount of money and have the potential to make so much money.

Compare this to any other business, and you will see what a bargain this is.

As excited as I am to tell you about the tools you need in this business to succeed that I have used to succeed in this business let's move on to the next chapter so I can tell you how I stumbled upon the secrets of selling products on the Internet.

HOW I SELL THOUSANDS OF PRODUCTS FROM HOME USIING THE INTERNET

How I Stumbled Upon The Secrets Of Selling Products On The Internet

I didn't really set out to become an Internet guru.

I stumbled upon this business by accident and I was terrified of it. I will never forget this.

Before I started out in this business I was writing ad copy for a company in Dallas, Texas. The World Wide was brand new. One of my responsibilities for this company was to work as a consultant to assist them in their plans to make money with this new called the web.

Words started flying around the office like "Eudora," domain names," "search engines," "email," "internet marketing" and so forth. All these words were foreign to me.

I was asked to register a domain name. I had no idea what this meant and what I was supposed to do. I was really demoralized by the technology and this new thing called the web.

Because my company was deeply involved in the early days of the Internet I met a guy named Jonathan Mize who was writing a E-zine for this company on how to market online.

After a couple days the two of us became friends. Three months later we went on to do 120 seminars together across the U.S.

While working as a consultant for this company I also met Declan Dunn who was a talented web designer and a expert in how to do affiliate marketing.

After three months of working together with these guys I learned the ropes of selling on the web.

Both these guys taught me that to make money selling products on the web all I had to do was write a sales letter for a product, upload it to a web page, get people to come to the web page, read the sales letter and click the order link.

After I created a sales letter and uploaded it I set up a merchant account so I could process credit cards and would you believe it my web site was making sales. I made many mistakes in the early days trying to sell products on the web but you can avoid these mistakes because of my experience.

After I set up my sales letter and my product I was making a few thousand dollars a month in sales with my product and sales letter. Three months later one of my products really hit and I started making $10,000-$20,000 in sales a month. My sales keep rolling in.

Jonathan Mizel and Declan Dunn showed me the basics of selling online. Since then I have been able to show thousands of people around the world the basics of selling online.

The mistakes I made in the early days of selling products online was expensive and a slow way to learn but because of my experience you can avoid these mistakes.

It is so much easier to avoid mistakes when you have someone pointing out the steps to take, steps to avoid, what software to buy, what order to do the steps in, where to host inexpensively and so on.

I am here for you. Based on my experience I am here for you. I am here to show you the ropes of this business so you can duplicate my sales.

It's a funny thing and like Deja Vu to grasp but registering a domain and ftp'ing files were scary at first but were actually easy once I learned how to them.

My fear was really for nothing.

With your okay I want to take you deeper into the ways of selling products and services on the Internet. I want to take you inside and show you how this business really works.

I want to show you how you can really make money.

I want to show you how you make money even while you sleep at night.

I know this is possible.

I do it every night.

I am going to show you how.

If I can do this business, you can too. I am not a computer genius but make lots of money selling online and it does not take a computer genius to do this business.

I do one thing well – write sales letters and it does not take a genius to do this either.

I have my successful sales letters boiled down to a simple formula and coded into software so that you can do it also. You will learn this later.

So here we go on to the next chapter.

HOW I SELL THOUSANDS OF PRODUCTS FROM HOME USING THE NET

Walking Through My System Step-by-Step

This is how I make money online:

1. **I get visitors to my web site by paying out commissions**.

I talked about this process earlier. In internet terms it is called an associate or affiliate program.

An example is http://www.bluelightalarm.com/.

When someone sells one of my products I pay them a commission.

The whole process works on a funny little word called "cookies." It is not something you eat. The first time I heard the word used, I literally thought it was a joke. To my amazement I later learned it was a real Internet word!

Here is how it works. You copy one of the banners off our tools page and put it on your website.

Anyone who clicks on that banner sets a cookie. What does that mean? A very small text file is written to their computer. When the visitor goes to the order form and fills it out to buy a product now, (or anytime in the future the ID number in the cookie text file is read, and the appropriate commission is applied to the owners account for that ID.

This ensures complete accuracy as to who gets credit for the sale.

Now I have to say that having your own associate program is only one way to get traffic. But for a lot of people it has turned out to be the best source hands down.

A really important note you need to know is that everyone wants to know HOW you get associates. The BEST way to do it is by turning every customer into an associate. I try to turn every customer into an promotionist for my products. And you should too.

Even if your customers do not have web sites, just about every customer uses email. They do have friends and family. Turn them into your informal sales force by creating a commission sales plan for them.

The other question I am always asked is how do you get associates when you do not have any customers? The answer is to post your offering in associate directories. Search under "affiliate directories" in any search engine and post your information in the different resources. All the ones I know of are free to post in.

By far the best way is to pick up the phone and make a phone call every time you see a web site that would be a good associate for your products.

2. **Use no-content web sites to make sales**

When I first started out I was a major advocate of the no-content web site. Just about everybody believes that your web site mush have a bunch of articles and information on it for people to buy.

In my experience this is a myth. My sales went up when I removed content from my web site. Later, experiment with putting content on your web site if you want to.

When you are first starting out, pretend your web site is like an envelope in cyberspace and inside are your cyber direct mail sales letter. This will surely get you lots of sales.

All my web sites are sales letters with order forms. This is what has worked for me. This has saved me a ton of time and money in trying to develop content that probably would not increase my chance of making a sale anyway. You need to do the same.

3. Use real time credit card processing

Real time credit card processing will process the customer's credit card immediately and check the card for fraud and theft and if the card is good.

If you are just starting out, I would recommend PayPal at paypal.com.

At this time, it is free to establish an account with PayPal.

4. Sell immediately downloadable, digitally-delivered products

You can sell all kinds of products on the Internet. I personally like courses, training materials, eBooks and software because they can be digitally delivered without sending a physical product. This saves time and money on shipping, returns, chargebacks and installation time. This also makes it much easier to sell to overseas markets.

It is really easy to create a eBook. You just type it up in Front page or Dreamweaver and sell it for any price you want. Add a zippy page design then you can use an eBook compiler like EBook Edit Pro or EBook Maestro Pro to compile your chapters into a downloadable eBook. The compiling process is a very simple process that literally only takes seconds. Anyone can do it.

When it comes to digitally delivering your product via download I would recommend
http://www.automateyourwebsite.com/.

This is a service that will charge the credit cards, issue a username and password and take your customers to your web page download site. This is a really cool service with a lot of features.

But if you want to create your own digital delivery system at a reasonable cost I would recommend hiring someone from elance.com. You can also use lance to find a graphic designer to help you with the design on your eBooks and web site.

This one resource everyone uses for eBook covers and graphics on websites is: Killer Covers.

You will find many other helpful resources at: http://www.therealstartpage.com/.

5. Follow up automatically using sequential autoresponders

After people buy you want to follow up and offer other products and services. This is called a upsell and will surely make you money. The method I use for this is called a sequential autoresponder which automatically sends a sequence of emails according to the schedule I specify.

Automateyourwebsite.com which I mentioned above has follow up autoresponders built into it. But if you want to create your own system, you can't go wrong with the three following sequential autoresponder services.

Get response. I have many autoresponders with get response.

Weber. I also use Weber and have found them to be very reliable.

ProAutoresponder. A new player on the block with a great pricing structure.

6. Hire and use independent contractors from elance.com

To get the best design, graphics, customer service and so forth, use the heck out of Enlace. I highly recommend it.

You cannot do everything yourself and lance is a great help. At Enlace, post the job you need help with. Then people around the world bid on doing it for you. This is an easy and cheap way to find help for your business.

Now that you understand my system step by step let's move on.

HOW I SELL THOUSANDS OF PRODUCTS FROM HOME USING THE NET

Failing to Spend the Money to Acquire True Specialized Knowledge

Mistake one: Failing to spend money to acquire true specialized knowledge

Because information is free on the Internet, some people confuse that information with specialized knowledge.

For example, let us say your are getting on a plane to take a trip overseas. Do you want to fly in a plane piloted by someone who read a free eBook on how to fly a plane? Or do you want the pilot to be someone who has gone through a real pilot training program?

You want the real deal, don't you? See, there is a big difference between free information and specialized knowledge of a skill or craft.

And this makes all the difference in the world.

Mistake two: Not understanding and utilizing the Mastermind process

In the book Think and Grow Rich the author Napoleon Hill explains the Mastermind concept and process. The Mastermind is about the power of collaborating with other people you trust on goals and projects.

After studying the richest people in America for over 20 years, Napoleon Hill determined that having a Mastermind group was the number one factor shared by rich people.

Do you have a team you can rely on? A team that backs you for your success? If not you really need to assemble one.

You want people on your Mastermind team who have businesses that are complementary to you, not competitive. Whereas competitors are not likely to openly and freely share their secrets, someone in another industry who is complementary to you can be a big help can be 100% on your side.

Mistake three: Not knowing how to get the money you need

To succeed in this business you are going to need money for your tools. Not a whole lot of money but just some money. The funds required for your online business are really fractional compared to most other businesses. You can succeed in this business with just a few hundred dollars. With just a little money you can get a huge return in investment.

You can save the money or take a loan on life insurance without borrowing a lot of money. Or use multiple credit cards or sign up for a new credit card and pay it off fast and get the credit card rating. Or take out a personal loan or bring in a partner or investor.

There are many ways to come up with the money you need.

Mistake four: Not understanding how you make a profit

Here is how you make a profit in this business and it is easy to do. You calculate your return on investment by dividing the money you take in by the money you spend to make that money. So in a month, if you spend $2,000 and make $9,000 your return or profit on the $2,000 is $7,000 or 333%.

Let's say you have to borrow the $3,000 for that month. And you pay 2% in interest to borrow that money. That 2% interest was a bargain because it allowed you to make much more.

What is the return on your money, on your investment? That is really the key. You must get out much more than you put in. When people and you get into trouble is when they make poor investments. When you put in a lot and only get out a little.

Learn to get your money returning high yields for you. This is the crust of the product selling business. This is what the product selling business is all about. You buy a product for X. Mark it up 4 or 5 times and sell it. That's a good return on investment.

Mistake five: Not following the proven formula for crafting a letter that sells

Do not reinvent the wheel on this one. I have spent a lifetime creating and perfecting this formula including research and client interviews. All you have to do is follow the http://www.pushbuttonletters.com/ formula for creating a successful sales letter.

I really want to stress the many websites I go to that deviate from this formula and therefore do not make any money. They forget to use this proven formula so they lose sales. Or, there is no way to order! Or the website does not present all the features and benefits of the product or service. Therefore, you cannot order because you do not have all the information you need. Many businesses just fail to follow these rules so they do not make any money.

Mistake six: Promoting multiple products on a page

Many websites I go to promote multiple products on a web page. I have found through research that this just confuses the user. I have found that the successful approach is to promote one product at a time. Everyone wants to create a catalog web site with all the products referenced on it. My experience has shown that this only confuses people.

The web really is a surfing environment. People surf many websites and are really impatient. You have only a minute to pull people into your sales process and sales letter. You only have a limited amount of time that the potential customer will spend at your web site. This is why you want to lead in with a sizzling offer any potential customer whose breathing cannot possibly say no to!

One way to attract potential customers is to use the appropriate colors. Blue on your website denotes confidence and trust. Red indicates danger. Also use action words like limited time offer, proven to perform, if we can't save you money what's the point and learn the one thing you need to know.

Then you follow up that purchase with other offers. Now you have the person on board as a customer. They have already spent money you. The follow up sales will be easier.

Mistake seven: Not finding the demand – first!

The mistake most beginners make in this industry is to start with a product before they know demand. Then they buy my courses to find out how to get people to buy their product!

This is exactly opposite of the way you do it.

First, you get the know how so you do things right to begin with.

Second, you find out the demand -- what people want. You always locate the demand first. I do this using surveys. And by talking to my customers and prospects.

Third, you test the waters on a small initial basis to verify people do indeed buy what they said they would. Sometimes people will say they want one thing and yet spend their money on another item. The ultimate vote is the pocketbook. Where do they spend their money?

Mistake eight: Not testing small

This is something people always do. People sink a fortune into a business or into inventory before they verify that people will buy the products. Absolutely do not take other people's word for it. Test the products yourself on a small basis first before you buy much at all in the way of inventory. And even then, start low and go slow. Do not load up until you really have to.

Mistake nine: Not understanding risk

When you start a business, you're taking a risk. There really is no other way to slice it. Do not invest money you cannot afford to lose. Not that you can ever afford to lose money. But understand that in business and life there are no ultimate guarantees.

Make no mistake. There are landmines in starting a business. What we do is show you the path we walk daily THROUGH the mines. Step in our steps. Do as we do. In this course I show you how to avoid the mines.

Mistake ten: Always preparing and never doing

A easy trap to fall into is preparing endlessly and never doing. You want to read my materials and courses. To learn what you can. But the you must DO. You will never make a profit if you do not offer that first product for sale!

Do not fall into the trap of thinking: "Only other people can do it. They are smarter. They are more talented. They are special." The most important thing in this business is probably just a sixth sense about what people want to buy. That has nothing to do with education or anything else.

The secret to this business is selling people what they want to buy. If you have a good gut feel for what people want to buy, you keep your expenses low, you make cheap mistakes (vs. expensive ones), then you have a good chance of surviving and thriving.

Mistake eleven: Taking counsel with the wrong sources

In this business, anyone can publish an eBook. Many are written by people with no real world business experience. Kids in the back rooms of their parent's houses and so forth. Don't fall for these traps.

You want a eBook written by someone with experience and counsel. You want to take counsel with proven business leaders who have been down the path you want to take. Free or cheap advice is some of the most expensive advice you'll ever get. Mistakes are far more expensive than the cost of sound business counsel.

Mistake twelve: Buying business opportunities that are supposedly ready-to-go moneymakers

You and I have never met.

Yet, I know what you want.

What you want is for me to hand you a business for a grand or less that you can make $100,000 a year within 40 hours a week or less. A business you can start with only a small amount of cash. And one that doesn't have much risk in it. One that is almost guaranteed to make you money. A business which is like a franchise with phone support, coaching and everything.

Well, I have to say I'm sorry. But that is a pipe dream.

That's what you want. And chances are about 95%, if that is what someone says they're selling you, it's a big, giant puff of smoke with not an ounce of reality to it.

You want to hear you can make money in business without a lot of work. That I've already found the market, found the products, created the marketing materials, created the lead generation system and all that. And you're going to make 100 g's your first year – no learning curve – almost guaranteed.

It's not going to happen.

You mark this down right now.

Douglas told you: "You are your own Easter Bunny, Fairy Godmother and Santa Claus. You are the creator of your own business opportunity, work-at-home plan and make-a-fortune system. Thank you very much."

If you want it to happen for you, then you've got to do it yourself. Nobody is going to hand you a money machine for a small investment. I don't care what they say. The sooner you get that straight, the sooner you're on your path to making money in this business.

And the sooner you stop chasing pipe dreams and jousting windmills.

The one proven path to success is learning marketing yourself.

Do not fall for someone's line that they're going to sell you a business for a song and dance where all you do is flip on the switch and it makes money.

More often than not, you will end up on the short end of that stick.

There are plenty of these offers out there that are a scam and only waste your time and money. The best advice I can tell you is for you to learn marketing yourself from someone like me who is an expert or from an expert in this field. Just type internet marketing experts in any search engine to help you.

Let me be clear here: I'm NOT slamming mom or network or network marketing. First of all, I'm primarily referring to business opportunities that charge you $1,000 to $20,000 for what is advertised and promoted as a turnkey business.

In reality, the business model doesn't work. Why? Because the company doesn't have a way to generate leads and turn them into sales that really works.

Yes, they will have success stories they can point to. A few. More often than not, these success stories are from people who have a great deal of experience in the field. Or they have advantages you don't, like a pre-existing customer base and so forth.

I am not against network marketing.

Some of my best friends have done quite well in it.

Having said this, I will also tell you that these friends have acquired a great deal of skill and knowledge about marketing. In other words, you STILL need to know marketing.

While companies put a great deal of time and money into creating marketing systems, my exposure and experience tells me the most successful distributors still create their own marketing systems.

Or if nothing else, their marketing training helps them use to the fullest potential the tools provided by the companies.

The reason people can get by with selling business opportunities that do not work is that people blame themselves for their lack of success.

What the truth is is that the company did not supply a workable way to generate leads and make sales. That's why I create the products I do. To train you how to generate your own leads, your own website visitors and make your own sales.

Then, in essence, you become your own business opportunity generator. You know how to do it yourself.

Then you don't need someone else.

This is why I say self education is absolutely necessary. The bit of information you just read could easily save you losing $5,000 or $10,000 on a bogus opportunity.

The best investment you will ever make is in your own training. And in developing the specialized knowledge and skills you need to succeed.

Some of my courses sell for $1000 to $3000. People who don't get it wonder how I can sell training for so much money. The reason is because it's an investment in your future. You can either rely on someone else to do it all for you. And pray to God they're honest. Or you can learn how to do it yourself.

My friends in this business spend $7,000 to $10,000 per year on education and training. That is what I spend.

You can never know too much about marketing nor be too skilled at it. That is why I continue to educate myself.

With this in mind let's move on.

HOW I SELL THOUSANDS OF PRODUCTS FROM HOME USING THE NET

How I Started On a Shoestring

When I started selling my eBooks online, I didn't have a fortune to spend. Basically, I did it on a shoestring. By that I mean for under $500.00

Here's how you start on a shoestring:

Secret one: Sell eBooks or other products and services that don't require the purchase of inventory.

You can use manufacturers that ship products directly to the customer for you. This is called dropshipping. You don't pay the manufacturer for the product until After the customer has paid you.

Inventory is one of the big cash guzzlers that can kill you. By using dropshipping, you can save yourself a lot of money in the beginning.

My route was to create and sell eBooks. But you are not limited to eBooks. You could, for example, sell a service. Again, no inventory required.

Secret two: Do not spend money on advertising until you know if you have a winner on your hands.

As I have already explained, I like to sell through resellers (also referred to as affiliates or associates). This way, I don't have to spend money on advertising.

What you do is contact web sites that could benefit from selling your product or service for a tidy commission and ask if they are game. Not everyone will say yes. But chances are, some will.

Another really good thing to do is to promote your associate program by submitting it to directories as explained earlier.

Secret three: Don't spend a lot of money on software. Software is expensive and so much of it does not work as advertised. I recommend you stick to the basics. Your ftp program, html editor (Front Page or Dreamweaver) and so forth.

Secret four: Do not spend a lot of time on creating a product until you know if it will sell. So many people spend six months or a year on a product that is a dead duck. You may have to try 7 times before you hit a winner. Time is money.

First, you validate demand. Then you expand the product. That means, if you are selling an eBook, first create a quick-and-dirty version of it. Write your killer sales letter and then get some promotion going on it. If it sells, then spend some time expanding the product. If it doesn't sell, go on to your next idea.

Secret five: Save your money and work at home. Many very successful businesses have been started from home initially. It is a great way to cut overhead to the bone.

Secret six: Spend what you can on training. Solid, practical training will speed your success greatly and help you avoid a ton of potential mistakes. Money spent on your own training is a great investment.

Secret seven: Test small and expand slowly. Do not sink your life's savings into one project. What you do is start small. Test. Find out that people Will buy your product or service. You do this by signing up to forums and doing surveys and asking friends and associates if they will buy the product or service you have to offer. If not, then move on the next product or service. Expand on this as you have the cash flow to do it.

Secret eight: Learn the skills you need for this business. Buy Front Page or Dreamweaver and learn to use it. Buy some marketing books or marketing eBooks or the ultimate sales letter books or subscribe to a internet marketing newsletter by a leading expert like mike Filsimaine or buy training CD's on these subjects or free online tutorials on these subjects.

Learn how to use your computer. There are plenty of books at the book stores on this.

Secret nine: Start your business part time. Go full time only as you have the money for it. I see a lot of sharp people start a business when they are broke and have no job.

If you have to do that, my advice is to start a service business where you can make cash flow from day one.

This is what I did. I did freelance writing to bring in cash. Later, I got paid to do public speaking. Both of these were services I provided to bring in cash while I got my product business up and running.

As I am excited you are reading this chapter I am equally excited for you to move on to the next chapter. So let's get to it.

HOW I SELL THOUSANDS OF PRODUCTS FROM HOME USING THE NET

How To Come Up With Your Product Ideas

One of the reasons people fall for business opportunities is they have great appeal:

We have products people want.

We have proven ads. You do not have to write anything.

We have the web site done for you.

We have lead generation or traffic methods already done for you.

All you do is plug it in and it makes money.

You are in the driver's seat when you don't need someone else to do it for you because you know how to do it yourself. Now, is learning how to do it yourself necessarily cheap or easy?

No. It is going to cost you some money. It is going to cost you time. But is it worth it? Absolutely. It's the only way to go.

Let us start your training right now by giving you several ways to find your own products.

One: Most of the companies in simplx will drop ship according to the information I've seen. This is an outstanding source of products.

Two: Look at what is ALREADY selling.

You do not have to blaze new trails. Look at what people are already buying and spending money on. Now, come up with your own new, improved version of those products and services.

Some of my friends created the product The Amazing Formula That Sells Products Like Crazy and there were already many products being sold on somewhat similar topics. What they did is add an angle. In the case of The Amazing Formula, they sold the product as a 100% digital download. No one else was doing this at the time.

That angle or uniqueness made the product a huge hit.

Three: Ask yourself – what is the next step?

Find a product that is really hot. Look at advertising on television or look at amazon.com for products that are really hot or are selling. After this Ask yourself, "after people buy this product, what is the very next thing they need?" Sell them that "next step" product.

So many people are advocating content-rich web sites that require big staffs (and overhead) to maintain. I say screw that. People are an impatient breed. You only have a minute to catch the web surfer's attention before they move on. What you want to do is sell something. Lots of content rich sites are a waste because the web surfer will not read it and move on and a waste of money on overhead. Just create a simple sales letter and a order form for your website

Four: Ask yourself – what product do YOU want to buy that is not available?

Create it, make it or find a supplier. If you are representative of a large group of people with a common vocation, interest or hobby, you could have a real winner on your hands.

Five: Turn complaints into gold.

What are people complaining about? Could you provide a solution to their complaint? Will they pay for the solution? One way you can find out is by testing small.

So many of my friends have a killer course on how to write sales letters. They found out that no one thinks they can write. So they came up with a software program where you just fill in the blanks and it practically writes the sales letter for you. Their product is called Push Button Letters. This idea turned out to be another huge seller for them.

Six: Revive old, abandoned products.

Look in magazines that are 5 years old for products that are no longer sold. Chances are, someone has a pile of those products in garage or storage somewhere. If you are lucky you may be able to snag the whole supply for almost nothing or for a modest royalty on sales.

Seven: Answer the "wouldn't it be great If" question.

Have you ever said, "wouldn't it be great if…" Of course you have. Now, provide the answer to wouldn't it be great if, and you could have a terrific little seller on your hands.

I had a problem. People bought my eBooks but did not know how to download them. Nowadays, this really is not a problem. But several years ago it was. So some of my friends created a product called The Ultimate Beginners Guide. The product contains practical tutorials on all the basic things computer beginners need to know how to do like ftp'ing files, zipping and unzipping, and so forth. It has been a steady seller for them.

Let's move on.

HOW I SELL THOUSANDS OF PRODUCTS FORM HOME USING THE NET

Is This Business For You?

I love my business. I love my life.

I wouldn't have it any other way.

I sleep as late as I want.

Go to the gym anytime I feel like it

Call my friends when I am in the mood.

Message my schedule so I don't drive when it's rush hour.

It is a great life. I don't have a boss breathing down my neck. If I fell like procrastinating, I do it. If I don't want to do it at all, I hire someone else to do it or simply scratch the project. I can travel because my schedule is flexible. I have more freedom than most people.

At the same time, having your own business is not a piece of cake. Don't get me wrong.

Are there long hours sometimes? Absolutely.

Is it frustrating when things are not going your way? Absolutely.

Do you risk losing money? Absolutely.

Does everyone succeed in this business? No.

Do the majority of people who try this business succeed? I don't know the answer but probably not. Although, I bet the number of people who really do their homework, buy and read the available training products and then follow instructions is pretty good.

Nothing is guaranteed. That is the real world. And anyone who tells you differently has a hidden agenda.

I am not a born business person. I suck at accounting and numbers. Truly I do. I was not good at writing sales letters in the beginning. I have friends who are much more skilled than I am at figuring out what people want to buy.

The main reason I have succeeded in this business is because of desire. I just wouldn't give up.

One of my favorite books is *Think and Grow Rich* by Napoleon Hill. Many years ago, Andrew Carnegie, founder of the steel industry in America, commissioned Napoleon Hill to study the richest people in America and write a summary of his findings.

The result of that research is the perennial best-selling book *Think and Grow Rich*.

Napoleon Hill found 17 keys to success which include the following:

1. Definite of purpose: You have to know specifically what you want and go for it. No room for wishy-washy stuff here. Be definite and resolute. This IS what I want. This IS what I will do. Part of this is the ability to TAKE ACTION.

2. Burning desire: You focus in with 100% clarity on what want.

3. Specialized knowledge: You acquire the specialized knowledge and skills it takes to succeed in your chosen endeavor.

4. The Mastermind: Teaming up with those who can help you succeed.

If you have the definite purpose and burning desire, my purpose is to give you the specialized knowledge you need as part of your Mastermind team.

I have dedicated my life to creating the training materials and courses people need to sell their products and services successfully. I would be honored if you give us the opportunity to assist you with building your business and taking it to the level of your own personal financial freedom.

5. Ability to make good decisions and take action:

I'm paraphrasing some here. But Napoleon Hill said that one of the key success factors was being able to make decisions and take action. A lot of people get the paralysis of analysis. They think about it. Think about it. Plan for it. And so forth. But they never act. They never "just do it" in the words of Nike.

Some people are just dreamers. They dream about having their own business. But they never get started. They never take the next step. That won't hack it. You have to be proactive. You have to be a doer if you want to be successful in your own business.

HOW I SELL THOUSANDS OF PRODUCTS FROM HOME USING THE NET

Everything I Promised In The Sales Letter

In the letter you read when you bought this product, I promised to reveal certain things. I now want to cover bullet by bullet every point I have promised to. Many of these have already been covered in the product.

But I want to put all the answers in one place for you, so you know I have covered everything and have fulfilled what I promised when you purchased this product.

Can you make a living online?

Do I make a living online? Yes. Do I have many friends in this business who do? Absolutely. Do many people I don't know make a living online? Yes, Can you do this? That depends on you; Do you have a definite purpose like Napoleon Hill talks about? Do you have a burning desire? Do you have or will you get the specialized knowledge and skills it takes to make it in this business? Will you persist until you succeed?

What products or services should you sell?

What I create and sell are information products like the one you are reading right now. I really recommend them because you do not have to ship or mail anything. You can also sell products that are not available to people locally. If someone can buy a product down the street for the same price you're selling it on the Internet, chances are they'll buy it down the street. However, if you can save people money, you can sell about anything. If you go to https://www.simplx.com/ and look at all the things being sold online there, you'll see that statement is true.

How much do you charge for your products?

The way you find out how much to charge is by testing different price points. You can create a rotating web page with two versions of your sales letter. One at one price and one at the other. I also look for what I call "holes in the marketplace." I look for price points no one else is selling at. If everyone in the market is selling cheap, I sell at a higher price. If everyone is selling expensive products, try the lower end or middle range.

How do you take orders?

What you do is set up real-time credit card processing. You can take credit cards using a merchant bank. You will find some of these on our web site therealstartpage.com.

Or you can use a service such as revector or PayPal. Once your account with Revco or PayPal is established, you can get the "Order Now" button on your site within minutes. Just copy the code they give, and paste that into your webpage where you want the order button to appear.

How do you take credit card orders?

The easiest way is to use a service like http://www.automateyourwebsite.com/. It automates everything for you. You can also hire a programmer as we did and set up your own custom systems. Just add a small piece of HTML code to your web page that generates the "Order Now" button for you. Anytime someone clicks on it they will be taken to your order form.

How do you deliver your products?

The automateyourwebsite.com software will handle digital delivery for you. If you have products you need to ship, see the resources on therealstartpage.com.

Is there still room for you online?

This is no different than any other business. There is always room at the top. When you read *Think and Grow Rich*, you will know why this is so. The secret to success is targeting a niche or area where you have an advantage over larger businesses. In other words, specialize in an area.

How do you make a six-figure income?

Break your income goal down into monthly and weekly goals. Plan on cash flowing 20% to 30% of gross sales. That means you need to gross $400,000 to $500,000 to make $100,000. If you run a lean, mean business and keep your expenses down, you can cash flow 50%. I have friends who do. That means you would only need to gross $200,000 to $250,000.

This is something most people build up to over a few years. Do not expect to gross that much your first year. If you do, you have exceptional abilities.

How do you run a business from home?

You have to sell digitally delivered products like eBooks or software. Or find someone else who will inventory and ship your products for you. This can be a manufacturer who dropships. Or it can be a service.

If you go to any search engine and look for "fulfillment" you will find many companies who inventory and ship products for a fee. To start out I do not recommend you start an inventory-type business because you are likely to get stuck with a bunch of products you can't sell.

Start with products you can obtain on a dropship basis. Or sell digitally delivered products.

How do you put up a web site?

Right now, the top html editors are Front Page and Dreamweaver. Of course, things do change. As you get in the business, you will know what tools people are using.

You can learn the basics of using Front Page or Dreamweaver in a weekend. It's pretty easy. They work pretty much like a word processor. You insert a table and type. You insert pictures. And so forth.

Once you're finished, you will need a place to host your web pages. This is called a web host. A web host leases you space on their computers that delivers web pages when people type in a urn (web site address beginning with www. You will find web hosts listed on therealstartpage.com.

Once you've signed up with your web host, you use a method called ftp to transfer the files to your web site.

What types of products are easiest to sell on the PC

I have pretty much already covered this. You can sell eBooks and software or products that are not easily available locally. Don't try to compete with Wall Mart. You need to sell products that people can Not buy locally. Or where you can sell at a 25% or greater savings vs. what people can buy locally.

Where to find products you can sell

Try https://www.simplx.com/ or http://www.dropshipdesign.com/ or http://www.productsourcing.com/. And read the chapter on coming up with product ideas.

How and where to find customers

The easiest way is to start an affiliate or associate program as we have discussed in the product. You can also use a pay-per-click search engine like overture.com.

How to deliver software and eBooks digitally – so you don't have to mail anything

The easiest way in the beginning is to use the software at: http://www.automateyourwebsite.com/

How to get other people to inventory and ship physical products for you, so you do not have to junk up your house

We have already talked about the dropshipping process. You can also use what are called fulfillment companies. Just search on the Net under the key word "fulfillment." You might even find a company in your own city or province that offers this service. Check your local phone book.

My 6-step hyper drive sales system

I've covered this in chapter six.

How to get dozens or hundreds of people selling your products for you

I have already talked about affiliate programs (also referred to associate or reseller programs). When you have your own affiliate program, you pay others a commission for selling your products.

How a friend of mine sold thousands of dollars of diamonds online

I haven't talked about this one yet. I have a friend named Kart. He is a very bright guy. He found some guys on eBay selling a web site that sold diamonds. They were making pretty good money at it even though the site was ugly and didn't incorporate many marketing methods like sales letters, autoresponders, and so forth.

Kart bought the site and the sellers hooked him up with their wholesalers and taught him about the business. Kart hired one of his friends for $10.00 per hour to be a phone sales person. He did quite well and sold the site for a big profit within one year.

How people make money with online auctions

The key to making money on eBay and other online auctions is in your buying. EBay is a price-driven market. If everybody and their dog are selling the same products you are for the same price, you have a tough business. Find a local supplier of products others aren't selling on eBay. Or that they are selling for considerably more money. I highly recommend you try https://www.simplx.com/

Why you don't need a big, fancy web site

People buy from sales letters. The marketing method that has worked for me is very simple. Write a drop dead sales letter for your product. Put it up on a web page. This is simple to do. Then drive traffic (that is, visitors) to your site using an affiliate program and pay-per-click traffic. You do not need a big, fancy web site. You need a hot sales letter.

How to sell stuff with emails

Once someone buys from you or signs up for your mailing list, you want to follow up with emails and possibly faxes. For example, my friend Kart offered weekly diamond specials. He would fax out a one-page list of these weekly to people who came to his web site and signed up for his mailings.

The automateyourwebsite.com software will allow you to place a form on your web site, so people can sign up for your mailing list. There are a number of autoresponder services listed at therealstartpage.com that will do the same thing.

The simple software I use

I have already covered software in one of the earlier chapters. Most of what you need is free or relatively inexpensive.

How to get started

Step one: Decide who you want to sell to

Step two: Create a list of 12 possible products and show it to people you identified in step one. Ask them to pick the 1 product they would be most likely to buy in the next 30 days.

Step three: Find a supplier for the product or, if it is a eBook, create your own quick-and-dirty version.

Step four: Write your sales letter.

Step five: Sign up for your web hosting.

Step six: Create an attractive web-page design for your sales letter.

Step seven: Decide on a method for taking credit cards.

Step eight: Place an order link on your web page that hooks up to your credit card system.

Step nine: Sign up for affiliate software.

Step ten: Create a sign-up page for your affiliates.

Step eleven: Announce your affiliate program to affiliate directories.

Step twelve: Call web sites that would make good affiliates and invite them to join your program.

HOW I SELL THOUSANDS OF PRODUCTS FROM HOME USING THE NET

Fifteen Tips Worth At Least $20.00 Each (And Probably Much More)

Tip One: How to make sales even if people do not read your sales letter. This tip WILL increase your sales and it costs you nothing. Plus, you can implement it in the next 30 minutes.

It's funny. I KNOW this. I have been a copywriter for a long time. But I forgot how important this was in online sales letters. Then, this weekend at a seminar, I heard my friend Terry Dean speak. He reminded me of the importance of subheads. People may not read all your sales letter. But they will skim your subheads. So work as hard on each subhead as you do the headline of your sales letter.

All you have to do to implement this idea is go through your sales letter and add attention-grabbing subheads.

A subhead is centered and in bold like this.

It grabs your attention.

Notice how all the tips on this page are worded in a way that gets your attention. This is exactly how you do the subheads on your sales letters.

Tip Two: How to have a perfect memory that obliterates information overload. Save tons of time searching for lost information and resources. Become a Brainiac in 10 minutes.

There is a ton of information you'll want to remember as you build your business. I cannot tell you how many times a day I use a little program that lets me type in and save notes then search for them later. The one I use is available at ZDNet and it's called *Easy Notre*. You can keep a daily diary in it. Plus, you can make notes that are instantly retrievable.

This is one of the best pieces of software I have ever purchased. It gives you the memory of a genius!

Tip Three: How to get drop dead graphics on your web pages for dirt cheap. Why pay thousands of dollars when you can get what you need for $100 -- $200 – or less. And it will often look better than graphics that cost a fortune.

There are several people now who specialize in doing top headers for web sites. These people don't charge much and create terrific graphics that load fast and give your web pages that pro look. You can find links to these sources at http://www.therealstartpage.com.

Tip Four: My amazing system for hiring people at a low cost who do all the hard work of my business and give me more free time to do what I want.

I use freelancers for every kind of project under the sun. I hire them from elance.com. What I do is this: I hire 3 people and give them sample projects. One will never finish the project (typically). One will do a so-so job of it. One will excel. I hire the person who excels to do more projects.

This little trick works for me every time. GIVE A TRIAL PROJECT TO THREE PEOPLE – ALWAYS. Never hire just one person for a project.

Tip Five: How to eliminate spam and viruses BEFORE you even download them. Save 30 minutes to an hour every day and save your hard drive from nasty viruses that can shut down your business for a week or more.

There is a new class of software that lets you actually view your mail on your mail server using Eudora or Outlook before you even download it. You can find a number of these programs at http://www.zdnet.com by searching on "spam filters." We have used one called *Quick Delete* and like it. Another one that looks good is called *Mail Sweep*. There are many of these programs available. And they are inexpensive. You NEVER want to download viruses to your computer. It's much smarter to delete them off the server.

Tip Six: The EASY way to split test your sales letters and web pages, so you know absolutely, positively which version creates the most leads and sales.

Split testing is where you test two different versions of a web page. One half of your visitors see one version. And the other half sees the other. This is the proven way to test headlines, sales letters and web designs to see which ones sell better.

At last, there is an easy way to split test your web pages. The product is at www.optinlightning.com. It has a built-in split testing feature. Plus, it allows you to track all your ads and tell you how many visitors and sales each one generates. There is another product at www.splithit.com designed for testing also.

Tip Seven: How to get web hosting for $2.00 -$3.00 per domain per month and save $20 to $30 per month on web hosting fees.

I've been happy using our web hosting from hostcentric.com. If you sign up for a reseller account, you can pay for 25 domains at a time and get them for only $2.00 - $3.00 each. At the time I'm writing this, they are $2.00 each over the monthly flat account fee. I say $2.00 to $3.00 because I assume the price will go up in the next one to three years.

Tip Eight: How to find the top resources for buying advertising. Plus, find out how your traffic ranks compared to your competitors.

Go to: www.trafficranking.com. You'll find that several of the top 50 web sites are in the business of selling advertising in the form of banner impressions, pop-ups, pop-under and so forth. Pop-ups are those ads that pop up when you go to a web site. Pop-under is ads that load in the background.

This site also lets you type in domains and find out the number of visitors that that site gets. You can compare the visitors to your web site with that of your competitors, assuming they are listed in the service. If you look at sites with a ranking similar to yours, you will get great joint venture ideas. That is, you'll find sites that might be willing to promote your products via an associate program.

Tip Nine: Where to get tons of free webmaster tools.

Here's a nifty site you'll love visiting. http://www.bravenet.com. It is loaded with free webmaster tools.

Tip Ten: How to get visitors to your web site if you don't have much money.

If you don't have much money, the best ways to promote your web site are as follows:

1. Start your own associate program. Nothing beats free. You don't pay out commissions until AFTER the sale. Turn every customer into an evangelist for your product.

2. Advertise on overture.com using bids from a nickel to fifteen cents. If you get 200 bids on decent key words in that price range, you should get some good traffic.

3. Pay for solo e-zine mailings. This is where an e-zine (newsletter sent out via email) sends out a standalone email for one of your products. These solo mailings have proven to be a good way to jump start a new business.

4. Write articles and submit them to e-zines. This is the equivalent of free advertising since you get to include your resource box at the end that gives the address of your web site.

Tip Eleven: Use ICQ, windows messenger, or yahoo messenger to communicate with staff and customers long distance. You save a fortune on phone bills this way.

These are great tools and we use them all the time in our business.

Tip Twelve: How to design your emails and web sites so people read them, thus increasing the likelihood they'll order and stuff your bank account with money.

Emails: Cut the line length off after 58 characters. Longer sentences are hard to read and can get screwed up in some email readers. Use CAPITAL LETTERS very sparingly. In the online world, capital letters mean you are screaming! Do NOT use a lot of!!!! or $$$$$ in your subject lines, emails or sales letters. This looks amateurish. Use the words "you" or "your" or here are your commissions in the subject line of your email or the headline of your sales letter if at all possible.

<u>Sales letters</u>: Sprinkle subheads throughout your sales letters. Write your letter with a real person in mind. Do NOT make your web site the equivalent of a brochure. Make it a personal, me to you letter. Keep the sentences on your sales letters under 17 words. Do not use more than 3 colors on a web page unless you know what you're doing. Use red sparingly in most cases since it's often associated with danger. Blue and green denote trust and reassurance. Do not use hot pink or other bright colors unless you are an experienced designer.

Tip Thirteen: How to come up with ideas for products to sell online.

Find a product that is selling very successfully. Then ask yourself, "What's the next logical step? What MUST the customer buy AFTER that product?" That could be your winning idea.

Tip Fourteen: Test anything and everything in a small way before you try to go big.

You pay more for small amounts, quantities and so forth. But it's often a big mistake to load up on anything before you prove the demand, supplier, system, resource and so forth.

Tip Fifteen: When you sign up for your merchant account, don't sign a contract for a hardware or software lease if you're selling on the Internet.

If you're selling on the internet, you will not be manually running cards, so you do not need hardware that allows you to do so. You don't need the vendor's software in most cases because you will be processing your cards through authorize net, Verisign or another such service. What the software does is allows you to manually process credit cards on your computer. But a payment gateway such as authorize.net or Verisign will process the credit cards for you real time. Therefore, you do not need software for that purpose.

This tip can save $1,000 to $2,000 that many merchant accounts try to charge you for. Others sell expensive monthly leases you do not need.

Tip Sixteen: Where to get a non-stop flow of online success stories each month for almost nothing. Why reinvent the wheel? Just use this resource to come up with business ideas that are proven to work.

In the U.S. there are a number of magazines published that target what I call the business opportunity market. That is, those who are interested in starting a business. If you are living outside the U.S., I imagine you can find similar magazines in your country, If not the ones I'm referring to.

Each month, these magazines feature articles of entrepreneurs making money in a specific business. These magazines are on major magazine stands in the U.S. The titles change over time. But look for titles like *Small Business Opportunities, Entrepreneur, Homebased Business Journal* and so forth.

HOW I SELL THOUSANDS OF PRODUCTS FROM HOME USING THE NET

What Else Do You Need to Know?

Obviously, in this introductory course, I can't tell you everything you need to know.

There are topics you will need in-depth training on to maximize your chances of success and your potential profits.

Topics such as:

- How to conduct surveys to find out what people want to buy
- How to write headlines that leap off the computer screen and make people read
- How to test your product ideas
- How to get associates
- How to maximize your chances of success
- How to avoid extremely costly mistakes

What I have done is put together a complete EBook training program that takes what's in my head and puts it in black-and-white for you.

Here is how to get the training you need

What I have done is put EVERYTHING in this eBook I thought you might need. You probably won't need everything in the EBook. I loaded it to the hilt so whatever you need is going to be covered. You'll see what I mean as I walk you through the EBook from the your money secret page.

Even though I created How I Sell Thousands of Products from home using the Internet I found out most people for whatever reason weren't actually doing it.

That is why I created the yourmoneysecret eBook page. And wow! Does it ever work? People tell us all the time in phone calls, emails and so forth how this eBook has helped them.

The eBook has no learning curve. Literally, all you do is read it, makes notes and apply the information.

If you are stressed for time and want a better understanding of the eBook read it and make notes at your leisure.

This concludes the How I Sell Thousands of Products From home using the Internet EBook.

If you follow this system you will make money.

By now you should have the best information possible on how to sell thousands of products from home using the internet from the number one leading expert.

Julius Caesar once said:

There is a tide in the affairs of men Which, taken at the flood, leads on to fortune; Omitted, all the voyage of their life Is bound in shallows and in miseries.

What about you?

Is this your tide? Is this your chance in life to take the flood at the crest?

Enjoy and Profit.

Douglas Fitzpatrick

www.best-value-electronics.com

Copyright © 2016 by Douglas Fitzpatrick

All rights reserved. No part of this publication may be reproduced, distributed, or transmitted in any form or by any means, including photocopying, recording, or other electronic or mechanical methods, without the prior written permission of the publisher, except in the case of brief quotations embodied in critical reviews and certain other noncommercial uses permitted by copyright law. For permission requests, write to the publisher, addressed "Attention: Permissions Coordinator," at the address below.

Best-Value-Electronics

P.O. Box 6836

McKinney, Texas 75070

www.ingramcontent.com/pod-product-compliance
Lightning Source LLC
Chambersburg PA
CBHW040332220526

45473CB00009B/2661